Pray CHURCH PRAY!

V. Michael McKay

Copyright ©2015 by Schaff Music Publishing, LLC
Houston, Texas | schaffmusicpublishing@gmail.com

All songs written by V. Michael McKay
Schaff Music Publishing, LLC (SESAC

Book layout, music transcription, & music engraving by Ricky Draper, EHD Music Services

Front cover photo, "If My People" by Ronnie Leviege
Editing by Paul Richard and Ellen McKnight

Back cover script by Michael D. Green
Cover design by Floyd J. Smith, FS Dezigns

ISBN 10: 0-9790785-8-X
ISBN 13: 978-0-9790785-8-3

ISBN 978-0-9790785-8-3

Pray Church, Pray!

Prayers have no expiration dates.

Many thanks to my brothers, Paul Richard and Mark Taylor, who collaborated with me through their submission of songs about prayer relevant to this collection. They dare to remind me of songs often forgotten. Their tirelessness of these texts and tunes point to the timelessness of the truths imbedded in these songs.

My mentor and sister in the faith, Dr. Margaret Pleasant Douroux, constantly challenges me. She continuously prays with and for me. She influenced the need for me to "write the songs down" when I had no clue of the importance of their documentation. Her love and prayers have proven never to expire.

My sister, confidant and encourager, Kathy B. McKay always stands in the gap for me—the times when I can't hear her voice are the times when I believe God can hear her clearly speaking on my behalf. The love and prayers of my mother, Helen I. Jones and my sister, Carolyn C. Cyrus, are paralleled to the love of God, the Father as expressed by a hymn writer, "His love has no limit…"

This book is dedicated to them, to whom I am forever grateful!

~**V. Michael McKay**

Pray Church, Pray!

Songs in this collection are all expressions of prayers to God, our Father, offered from the heart of a songwriter. Whether viewed as petition or privilege, prayer is essential to the life of the believer. Whether intercessory, on your knees praying for someone else, prostration, the act of personal submissiveness or worship to God, prayer is unavoidable for the believer.

Prayer is worship and praise.
I cried out to him with my mouth;
His praise was on my tongue.
Psalm 66:17 (NIV)

Prayer is worship and listening.
About midnight Paul and Silas were praying and singing
hymns to God, and the other prisoners were listening to them.
Acts 16:25 (NIV)

Prayer is corporate and constant.
They all joined together constantly in prayer, along with the
women and Mary the mother of Jesus, and with his brothers.
Acts 1:14 (NIV)

Prayer is timeless and non-negotiable.
Jesus told his disciples a parable about their
need to pray all the time and never give up.
Luke 18:1 (ISV)

Prayer is that and much more. Prayer is communication between the Father and His children. The expectation is that God, the Father listening and responding, and His children obeying and receiving.

"Pray Church, Pray! Put it all in His hand, because something is bound to happen when the church begins to pray!" This is my humble submission.

Your servant and co-laborer in the faith,
~V. Michael McKay

Pray Church, Pray!

When we come together in prayer, we are acknowledging the omnipotence, omnipresence and omniscience of our living God and Savior Jesus Christ. He communicates with us through our joys and fears, triumphs and lamentations, mountaintops and valley lows, while also providing a place for us to be still and listen in our most vulnerable hour.

We must pray to God just as we are, with broken words and broken thoughts. It is through those broken places that God will come in and close the gaps that have prevented us from healing. We talk to our friends, family, coworkers and doctors, but none of them are all powerful, all present, or all knowing; however, the Church does belong to the One who is. So "Pray Church, Pray!"

Don't worry about having the right words to say, don't worry about if it's the right kind of praise, don't worry about the chains that you cant seem to flee, and don't worry about having monetary things. The only worry that should consume our day is the reality of not taking more time out to pray.

~**Rennekia Goffney**

Pray Church, pray!

*If my people, who are called by my name,
will humble themselves and pray
and seek my face and turn from their wicked ways,
then I will hear from heaven,
and I will forgive their sin and will heal their land.*

II Chronicles 7:14

Pray Church, Pray!

Forward	3
Dedication	6
When the Church Begins to Pray	8
In His Place	12
Purify Me	14
Prayer Works	20
If My People	22
Oh Jesus	25
Integrity	26
Intercession	32
Talk to God	36
Talk to Me	38
Fix Me	42
All in His Hand	44

When the Church Begins to Pray

Acts 16

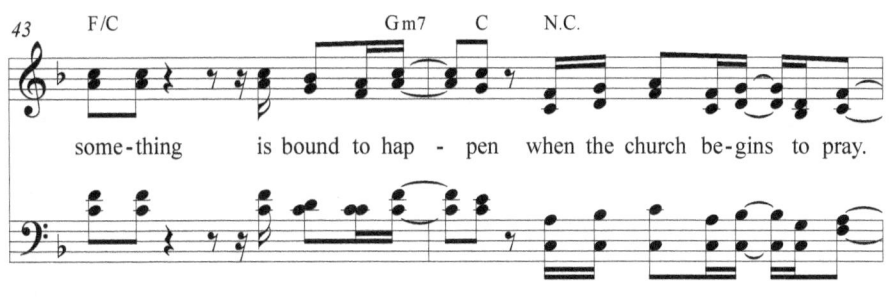
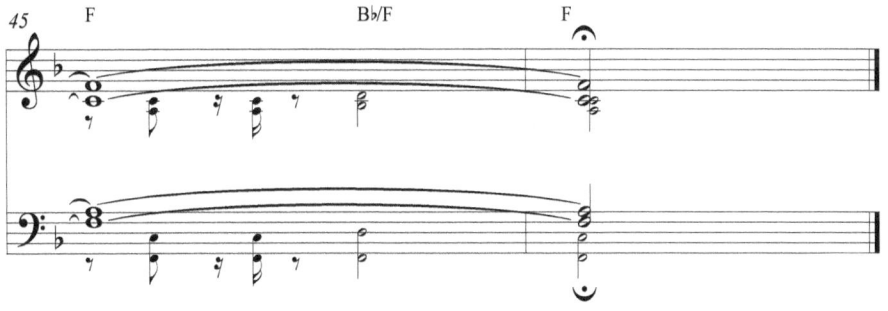

Purify Me

James 4:7-8

Moderate with expression ♩=60

Prayer Works

2 Kings 6:17-23

Uptempo ♩=140

Prayer works, prayer works, prayer works e-very time. Prayer works, prayer works, prayer works e - ver - y - time.

I'll keep pray - ing, keep on

If My People

2 Chronicles 7:14

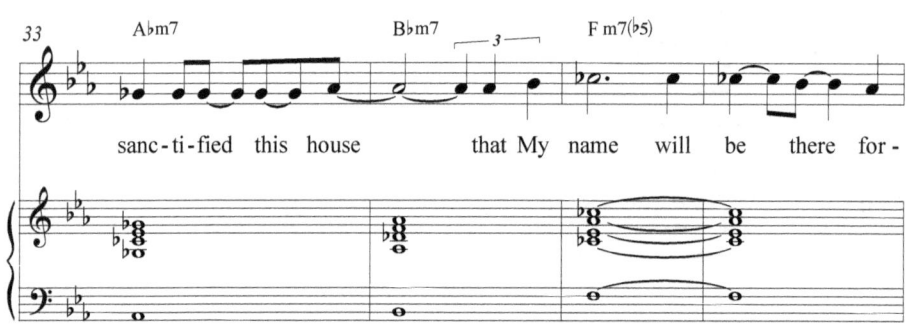
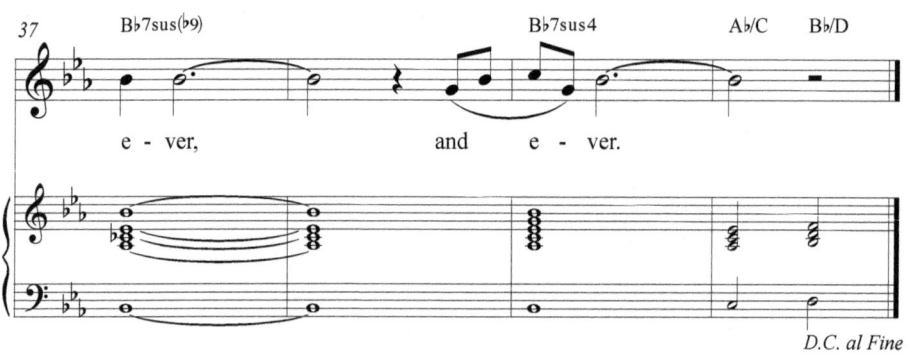

D.C. al Fine

INTEGRITY

Proverbs 10:9

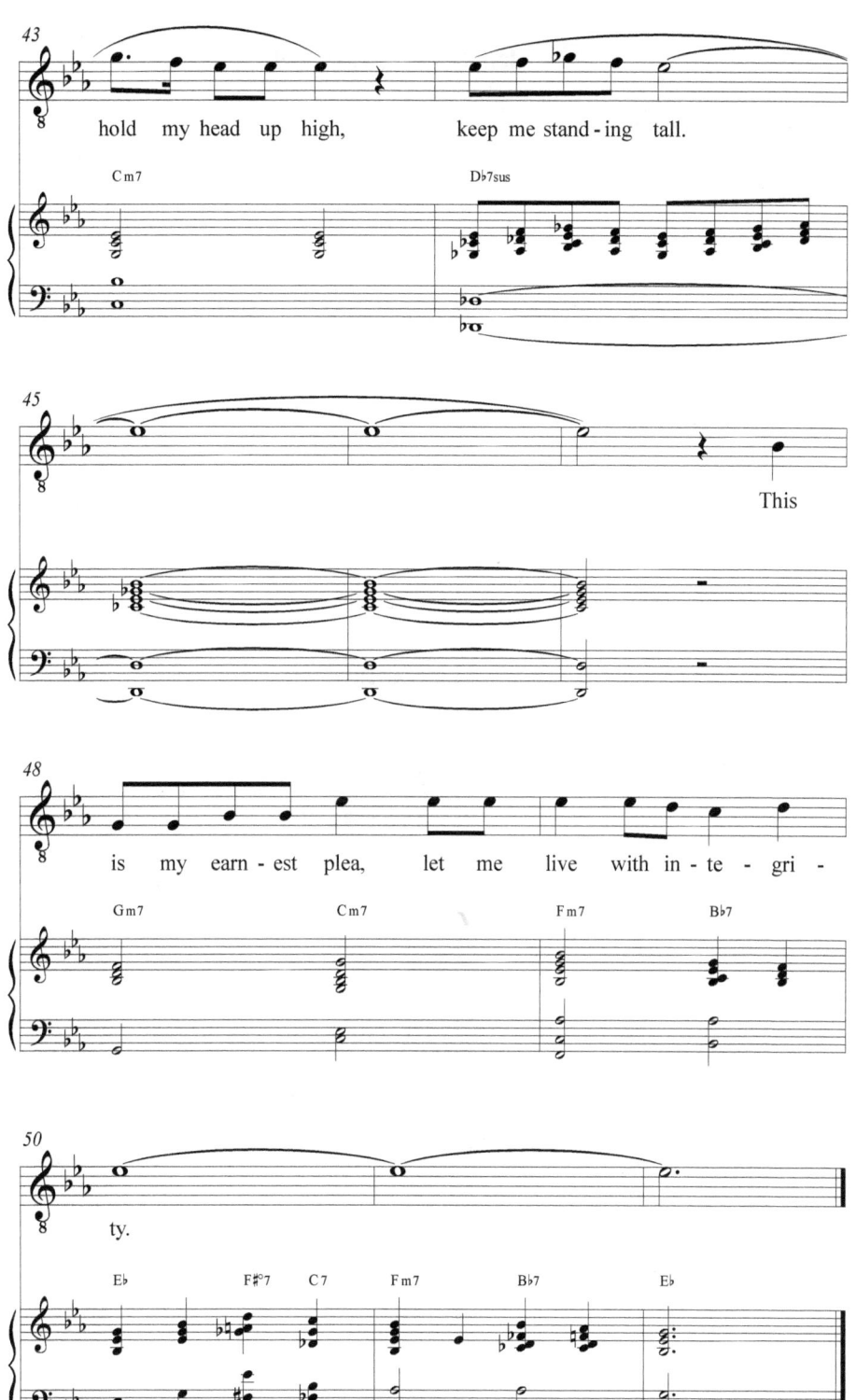

INTERCESSION

2 Corinthians 1:11

Slow and expressive ♩=60

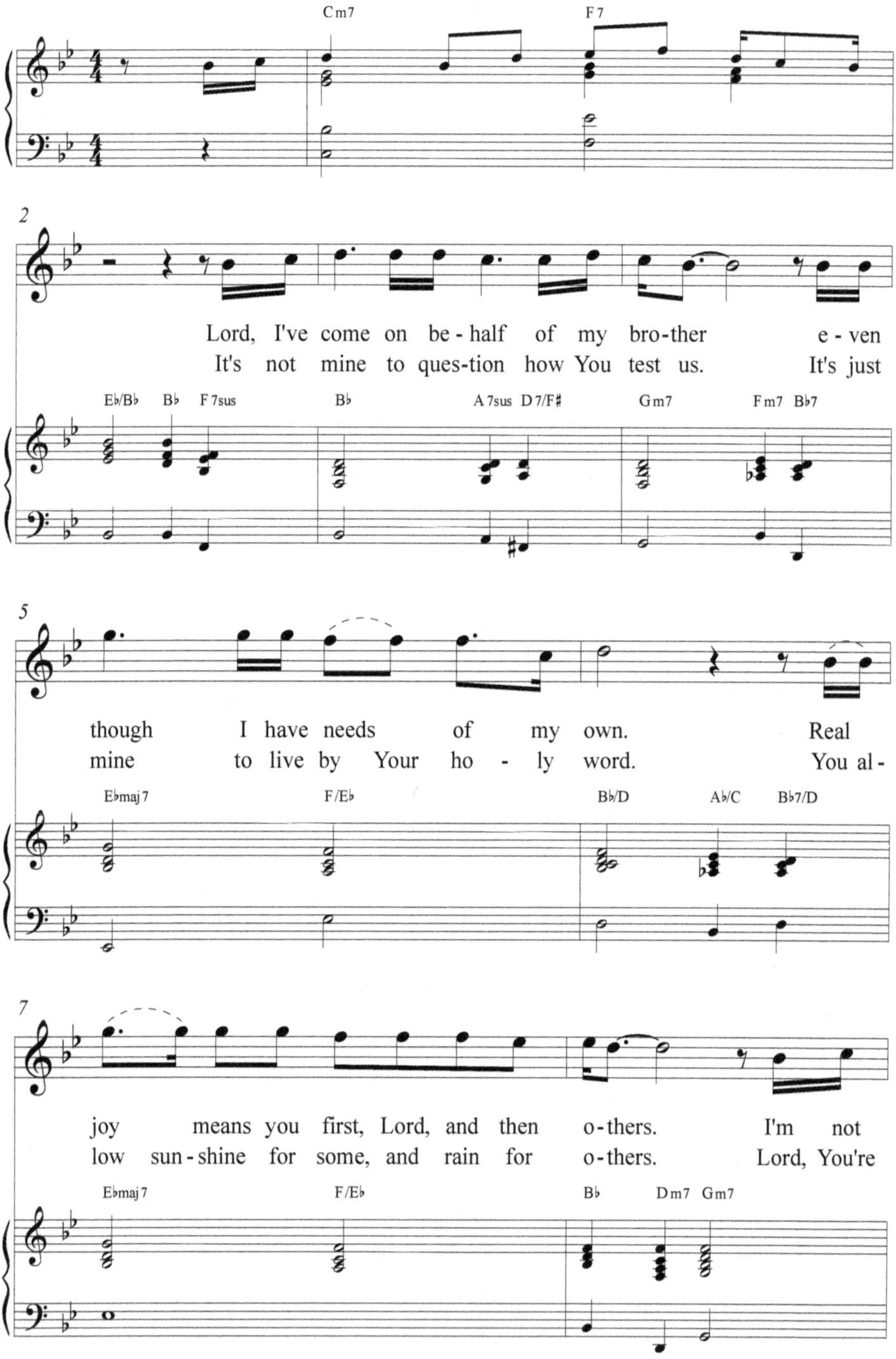

Cm7 F7
2
Lord, I've come on be - half of my bro-ther e - ven
It's not mine to ques-tion how You test us. It's just
Eb/Bb Bb F7sus Bb A7sus D7/F# Gm7 Fm7 Bb7
5
though I have needs of my own. Real
mine to live by Your ho - ly word. You al -
Ebmaj7 F/Eb Bb/D Ab/C Bb7/D
7
joy means you first, Lord, and then o-thers. I'm not
low sun-shine for some, and rain for o-thers. Lord, You're
Ebmaj7 F/Eb Bb Dm7 Gm7

Fix Me

Psalm 51

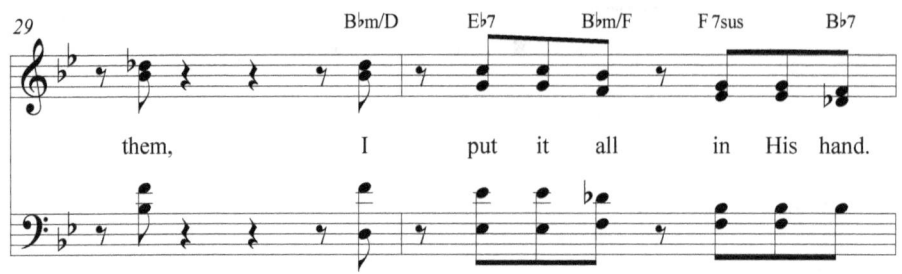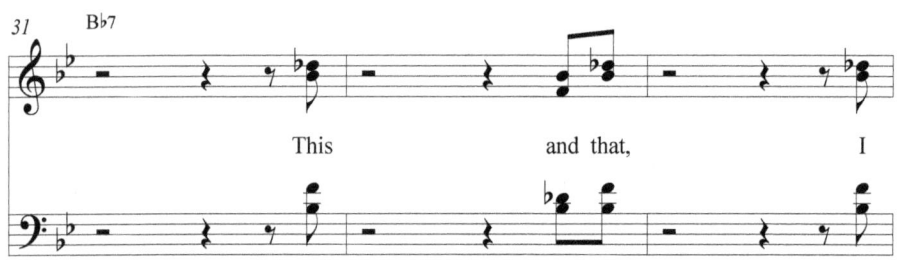

Other Books by V. Michael McKay

Hymns for HIM

This collection is the first of its kind—a hymnal containing 62 sacred works composed over a 40 year span from the pen of an individual African-American gospel composer, V. Michael McKay. Every song has a story, a testimony, or an experience which is retold in a rhythmic, musical form for congregations and singers to sing. The messages of Hymn for Him are inspired by sermons and church experiences.

God Talk

God Talk: Sounds of a Sanctuary is a collection of 13 songs from the pen of V. Michael McKay, whose language reflects the mind of God and echoes the voice of the church. Each song is a testament of timeless messages passed from generation to generation coupled with relevant sounds of today and is guaranteed be an interactive experience for believers of all age groups and backgrounds.

Flow in the Spirit

In the 21st century church, *flowing in the Spirit* has become synonymous with the "order of worship." The components still exist, but the language used to approach the total worship experience has changed. Within this collection of 11 songs, V. Michael McKay exhibits the language, the style, the rhythm, and the music of *flowing in the Spirit*.

From the Tabernacle to the Temple

The portability of the tabernacle affords an ongoing potential for something new and different. The permanency of the temple creates an awareness for sustainability and longevity. The transition from the tabernacle to the temple is evidence that God is still speaking. While in the temple, keep listening and looking for God. He is and will always be passing by. ~V.M.M.

I Would Sit Up with You, But I'm Sick Myself

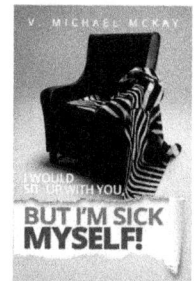

This book is in honor of those Christians who are honest enough to admit that they have been wounded on the playing field of ministry. I discuss some past healed scrapes and long-healed wounds of my own. I do so for the edification of Christians who operate within the body of Christ in church leadership roles. For the first time, I am openly admitting some of my feelings, thoughts and emotions to my ministry co-laborers. I hope that by the end of this book your awareness of a need for spiritual healing in the church, and all who have been touched by the church, will become very real. ~V.M.M.

Great Responsibility Behind the Wheel

"While driving, my grandfather challenged me when I became rowdy in the back seat of the car. I will never forget hearing him say, "Shut up little boy. There's *great responsibility behind this wheel."*~V.M.M. In this book, V. Michael McKay described the components of effective leadership and the great responsibility eadership carries. He carefully dissected each component, with regard to life experience, personal observations, and scriptural principles.

Life: A Continuum of Lessons

This collection of real life stories and quotes are highlights of formulas that have helped me throughout my lifetime. I am sharing them with you with hopes they will help lead you to a safe journey's end. This book is the inception of my legacy, The Legacy of V. Michael McKay, things that I purposefully and intentionally chose to leave. Otherwise, "How will you know I was here?" ~V.M.M.

And many more to come!

www.ingramcontent.com/pod-product-compliance
Lightning Source LLC
Chambersburg PA
CBHW050919160426
43194CB00011B/2473